MORE THAN CONQUERORS

The Power of Jesus' Blood, Cross and Name

Edward Thibault

The Word Among Us Press

9639 Doctor Perry Road

Ijamsville, Maryland 21754

ISBN: 0-932085-16-4

Cover design by David Crosson

Made and printed in the United States of America.

Contents

Introduction

Imagine a swimming competition in which the goal is to swim across the Atlantic Ocean. One swimmer is an Olympic athlete, well-trained and in perfect physical condition. The other is out of shape and has not even been in the water for several years. You would naturally expect the Olympian to be able to swim much farther and faster, but you still would not expect either of them to complete even a small fraction of the race. In fact, given the size and power of the ocean, both swimmers would eventually need to be rescued before they drowned!

We can compare this situation with our journey of faith. Some of us may be better able to pray than others. Some may have a stronger will or a more peaceful disposition. Others may feel incapable of overcoming temptation. Yet, like our two swimmers, on our own none of us is able—no matter how hard we try—to live a victorious Christian life. This is why Jesus died and rose triumphant over death. In him, all our sins and guilt are washed away and we receive the surpassing love of God. Through Christ, we can be filled with the Spirit's power to overcome situations that at first seem overwhelming. As Jesus assured his disciples, "All things are possible with God" (Mark 10:27).

In this book, *More Than Conquerors*, we look at three central truths which flow from Jesus' death and resurrection—the power of his blood, his cross, and his name. God has given us these gifts so that we can "run the race" and actually reach the finish line. As we learn to appropriate all that is available to us in these precious gifts, we can cry out with St. Paul: "I am sure that neither death, nor life, nor angels, nor principalities, nor things present, nor things to come, nor powers, nor height, nor depth, nor anything else in all creation, will be able to separate us from the love of God in Christ Jesus our Lord" (Romans 8:38-39).

May the Lord continue to pour out his abundant grace on all of us as we prayerfully pursue the riches of the knowledge of Jesus Christ (Colossians 2:2).

The Blood of the Covenant
Behold the Man

On the day that Jesus was crucified, there were probably only a handful of people who understood—even faintly—what was transpiring. We can think of the faith of the centurion (Mark 15:39) and the repentance of the "good thief" (Luke 23:42-43). We think too of Mary, who had known from the start that her son would bring salvation to the world (Matthew 1:20-21), and the beloved disciple who stood ready to receive Mary as his mother (John 19:26-27). Yet, for the most part, those who passed by that place of execution only saw three men being punished for crimes they may or may not have committed.

Two thousand years later, we too see Jesus on the cross—in our churches and in our homes—and we are invited to look upon him with the same faith that inspired Mary, John, the centurion and the repentant thief. With the eyes of faith, we can see the Father's heart as he gave up his only Son for our salvation. We can see Jesus' blood flowing freely, washing away our guilt and reconciling us to God. Gazing on our crucified Lord, we can rejoice in our salvation.

In this book, we explore three powerful gifts which God has given us in Christ—the blood, the cross, and the name of Jesus. Through these gifts, we can know freedom from sin, a share in Christ's victory, and authority over anything that challenges our trust in God's provision. The more we grow in understanding of all that is available to us in these gifts, the greater will be our experience of the Father's love and the Spirit's presence in our hearts.

The Blood of the Lamb

From their earliest days, the children of Israel had a deep reverence for the blood of all living things. To the Semitic mind, not only was blood essential to life, it was the seat of life's power. The Israelites understood that they owed their very existence as a people to an offering of blood. The story of their exodus from slavery in Egypt—recounted every year at the feast of Passover—would be incomplete without the tale of the blood of the lamb, placed on their door posts and lintels, which saved them from the destroying angel (Exodus 12:21-27).

Having escaped their bondage in Egypt, the Israelites traveled to Mount Sinai, where they entered into a covenant with God. They became Yahweh's special possession; he became their God—their protector, their provider, and their life-giver. In a solemn ceremony, Moses ratified this covenant in blood (Exodus 24:3-8), establishing a living link between the people and their God.

So deep was the Israelites' conviction that "the life of the flesh is in the blood" (Leviticus 17:11) that blood took on a central role in their worship—especially in rituals of atonement for sin. As the life-blood of a sacrificial animal was offered on behalf of a person who had sinned, that person's guilt and sin were washed away, and he or she was restored to membership in the community (Leviticus 4:27-35). At the pinnacle of such practices stood the annual Day of Atonement, when the high priest would make an offering of blood—first for himself and then for the people—which would remove all the guilt of their sins.

From Prophecy to Fulfillment

In light of the cross of Christ, we can see how Israel's blood rites served as precursor of the new covenant that Jesus established in his own blood.

At the last supper, as he offered the wine to his disciples, Jesus told them to drink it, because it was his "blood of the covenant, which is poured out for many for the forgiveness of sins" (Matthew 26:28). Similarly, St. Peter's letters tell us that we have been "ransomed . . . with the precious blood of Christ, like that of a lamb without blemish or spot" (1 Peter 1:18-19). The letter to the Hebrews contains what is probably the clearest teaching on the blood of Jesus, the blood of the new covenant, offered to free us from a guilty conscience (Hebrews 9:11-28).

As Christians, we believe that Jesus shed his blood to free us from sin and to re-unite us with the Father. Sin involves turning away from God. Because we all inherited the sin of Adam, we were separated from God. There was nothing we could do to bring us back to him. No good deeds or promises to try harder could ever remove our sin and guilt. This is why Jesus shed his blood—to reconcile us with the Father by releasing us from the power of sin and the oppression of guilt.

In the waters of baptism, we are immersed in the saving power of Jesus' death and resurrection. Now that we have been justified through baptism, the precious blood of Jesus is available to us every day, with the power to cleanse our consciences, unite us ever more closely to God, and overcome the lies of the devil. The letter to the Hebrews teaches that through the blood, we can approach God confidently, knowing that he will hear us and pour out his love on us (Hebrews 10:19-22).

Jesus' blood goes beyond simply washing away past sins. Because "the life is in the blood," his blood has the power to impart divine life to us, to heal and restore us. Often, when Jesus healed people, the healing was tied up with the forgiveness of their sins (Matthew 9:1-8; Mark 10:46-52). People in his day asked, "How can this man forgive sin?" Today, people ask, "How can anyone really expect to be healed by Jesus? Isn't that putting God to the test?"

Both of these attitudes reveal a human-centered view of God's divine action. God does not simply react to our needs or actions, as if he were waiting to find out what we wanted him to do for us. No, it is because of his perfect love that he created us, and it is because of this same love that Jesus shed his blood for us and daily pours his life into us. We might find it difficult to believe that God wants to heal and deliver us simply because he loves us. He shed his blood not only to wipe our slate clean, but to reunite us with God so that, filled with his love, we would love and serve one another in freedom and joy.

As with every other aspect of the gospel, it is the Holy Spirit's role to deepen our understanding and experience of the blood of Christ and its place in our life with God. Just as we could not win our own forgiveness, even so now, it is not our effort alone that will bring about a greater freedom from sin. Rather, our primary calling is to believe—to receive in faith and trust the gift of new life that God has already bestowed on us. Let us look at a real-life experience to illustrate this point.

There Must Be More

Mike is a retired government worker in his early sixties and father of five children. He had always prided himself on never having been sick a day in his life, until about three years ago, when he began to experience a series of medical problems for which he was hospitalized on several occasions. With each incident, the symptoms disappeared before the doctors could determine the cause of the problem. While Mike attributed these little "miracles" to the prayers of many of his friends, he knew that the underlying medical problem remained unaddressed and unresolved.

As they observed their reactions to these often frightening incidents, Mike and his wife Nancy began to realize that something was missing in their life of faith. They would pray to God for healing, and thank God when Mike was released from the hospital, but they felt they were missing the mark somehow. Mike saw that asking for a quick release from the hospital was like asking God to forgive him for past sins, yet not seeking a closer relationship with God. He was more interested in what God would do for him than in whether he could know God's love.

At the same time, Mike began to see that whenever he received the chalice at Mass, he would thank Jesus for dying for him, but never knew the power of this precious blood to fill him with divine life. The blood of Christ was little more than an intellectual exercise that couldn't stand up to the cold logic of medical science.

Within a week of coming to this realization, Mike was back in the hospital. This time the doctors found cancerous tumors in his liver. Mike began a treatment plan consisting of daily injections of medicine, which Nancy faithfully administered to him. Now, the time had come for Mike to test the truths about the blood that he had been thinking about.

The Power of the Blood Touching Our Lives

Together with Nancy, Mike began to pray regularly with some friends from church, asking God to open his heart more fully to the promises in scripture about the blood of Jesus. As he persisted in prayer, Mike noticed some remarkable changes. First, he saw that when he prayed, his anxiety about his future would give way to peace and trust. The sense of God's love became real to him and he began to trust that his heavenly Father was with him and would never abandon him. Even when he thought about death, Mike was at peace, because that only meant moving closer to the One whose love he was now experiencing.

When people asked Mike whether he believed

that God might heal him, he would reply that God had already healed him. If his condition worsened, the Father still loved him. If the cancer were to miraculously disappear, the Father still loved him. Nothing, neither death nor life, could change God's love for him. Jesus had offered up his life's blood for Mike—and for all people—and nothing could overcome the love that had motivated such a sacrifice. Mike realized that he was experiencing the truth of Jesus' words: "Your sins are forgiven. Get up and walk."

The power of the blood of Jesus had become more than a fine point of doctrine to be debated by theologians. Mike was experiencing that power in his own life, and he knew that physical healing was secondary to spiritual healing. He rejoiced in the Father's love and was able to worship God in a whole new way. The words of the various Eucharistic prayers took on a new meaning for Mike and Nancy as they came to understand more clearly all that was available to them in "the cup of eternal salvation," and "the blood of the new and everlasting covenant." Other people noticed the change in them and wondered how they could be so joyful in the midst of such a frightening illness.

The power of Jesus' blood to wash away sin and heal our lives is more than doctrinal theory. The people whom Jesus had forgiven and healed certainly knew that they were incapable of either accomplishment. Only Jesus, reaching out in love, could forgive and heal. They only had to receive his love and let it change their lives.

People frequently ask, "If Jesus were here today, what would he do?" But Jesus *is* here. He wants us to know his unfailing love and the power of his blood to free us. He wants to work in us, so that we live the new life he has won for us—a life of worship, a life of joy, a life of love. This is what we're destined to be doing for all eternity, and it has been secured for us in the blood of Christ, the Lamb of God, who takes away the sins of the world.

The Cross of Victory
The Key to Receiving God's Mercy.

When we speak of the cross of Christ, we often refer only to the pieces of wood that were used as the instrument of Jesus' death. But if we search the scriptures and read the writings of the Fathers of the church, we begin to see a much broader view, a perspective that includes the whole drama of our salvation— Jesus' incarnation, his death and resurrection, and his ascension into heaven. At its heart, the cross of Christ testifies to an outpouring of God's love that has the power to transform lives; this is the message we want to dwell upon.

All too often, we tend to look at the cross only

from the aspect of Jesus' suffering and death. We may think of how he was unjustly executed, or we may lament over the various "crosses" we have to bear in our lives. We may even have a view of God the Father as a relentless taskmaster who required the death of his Son, a cold, heartless judge whose primary concerns are justice and punishment.

But when we look at the cross in the light of the resurrection, and in the light of God's desire to draw all people to himself, we begin to see how Jesus' love for us moved him to offer up his life to bring us to salvation. With St. Paul, we appreciate the cross as "the power of God and the wisdom of God" (1 Corinthians 1:24). We see in the cross victory over sin and death, and the defeat of the powers of darkness—both in the world and in human hearts. This brings us to wonder: How can an instrument of torture and death actually bring joy to believers' hearts—even to the point of "boasting" in it (Galatians 6:14)?

The Cross as an Instrument of Death

As Christians, we are taught that our "old self" is crucified with Christ at our baptism (Romans 6:3). We are united with Jesus' death and resurrection so that we die to sin and rise with him to new life, freed from the power of sin (6:4-6). In Jesus' death, sin itself is put to death; in his resurrection, a new life of love and freedom is poured out. Just as Jesus shed his blood to win forgiveness for us, he offered up his life on the cross to free us from the power of sin. In other words, by the power of the blood, our *sins* have been dealt with; by the power of the cross, *we* are dealt with. We have been crucified with Christ.

This precious truth that the church has preserved throughout her 2,000-year history is one of Christianity's central boasts. Yet in our daily lives, we all can attest to the pull of the old nature enticing us to sin. How do we reconcile these two seemingly contradictory realities? Are Christians just hypocrites? Or is there more to the cross than first meets the eye?

Neither the power of the blood nor the power of the cross is a magical formula that we conjure up at will. Rather, our experience of the blood and the cross is based on *faith*. We believe it is true because God has revealed it to the church through his Son's death and resurrection. We believe it because Peter, Paul, James, John, and countless saints over the centuries have witnessed to this power in their lives and we see its fruit manifested in their words and deeds. Because redemption is God's gift freely given, flowing from a heart of boundless love, this power is freely available to all who are open to receive it. The power of the cross is not limited to spiritual "superstars." God wants all people to know this power in their daily lives. Christ has already done the work for us. Now, in faith, we can receive its benefits as we prayerfully ponder his love and seek to obey his commands.

The Challenge of Faith

Let's look at Mike and Nancy again, to see how the power of the cross applies in their situation. It was one thing to have experienced the blood washing them clean and healing them internally as they dealt with the complexities of Mike's cancer. But there were also times of quiet desperation, when pain or anxiety returned, when they felt more keenly a sense of being alone in the world.

Within a week of Mike's surgery, he was faced with painful conflict among members of his family. As a result of this conflict, and at a time when he felt he most needed it, Mike could no longer look to his older brother—who always had a good answer for everything—for strength and support. He could only look to the Lord.

As he sought to make sense of the division and strife in his family, Mike recognized old habits of judging and condemning others resurfacing in him. For her part, Nancy could detect patterns of fear in herself and a desire for retribution. They both saw how these patterns ran deep and, if left unattended, could taint what God had been doing in their lives. This is where the power of the cross was needed—to put these long-standing patterns to death so that, like St. Paul, Mike and Nancy would be crucified to the world and the world to them (Galatians 6:14).

An Accomplished Work

In the past, Mike would have gritted his teeth and tried harder to "die to self" when fears or bitterness would rise up in him. But as he sat at Mass, he began to understand some of the prayers in a new light. In the Memorial Acclamation, he prayed, "Dying, you destroyed our death; rising you restored our life." "Death" wasn't just physical death; it was also a living death of separation from God and others that was the result of sin. Jesus' death on the cross had done away with even *that* death. "Life" was a real possibility for him.

In the Prefaces of the Eucharistic Prayer, Mike heard the priest pray, "Through his cross and res- urrection he freed us from sin and death and called us to the glory that has made us a chosen race." "By his birth we are reborn. In his suffering we are freed from sin. By his rising from the dead we rise to everlasting life." So many other prayers—even the entire purpose of the Mass— opened up new horizons for him.

The Spirit was showing Mike that while his efforts at staying faithful to God had produced some wonderful results, something new was still awaiting him. God had *already* accomplished much for him through the cross, but Mike had often times felt that the struggle against sin was all on *his* shoul- ders, *his* battle to endure alone. Now, as he faced his cancer—a disease that went beyond his control— Mike saw that the time had come to let the Lord work. It was time to receive, just as he freely received Jesus' body and blood in the Eucharist.

Where Doctrine and Experience Meet

Over time, Mike came to appreciate how close the relationship was between doctrine and experience. As a young man, he had spent ten years in a seminary, until he felt the Lord calling him to a different life. He had learned a great deal of doctrine during that time, and it had been a beacon to him in later life. The truths that he learned were unshakable facts that provided an anchor and even brought him comfort at times. But doctrine had not changed his life; he had never really experienced the truth of the doctrine.

Now, in light of his growing experience of the Father's love, Jesus' salvation, and the Holy Spirit's power, Mike began to see how these doctrinal points fit into God's plan. The truths became alive to him, and scripture took on new meaning and power. And all of this was happening as Mike simply opened his heart to receive the love of God and allowed the cross to free him from anxiety about his future and resentment within his family.

God used Mike's physical and spiritual battles to teach him about his need for the power of the cross in his life. While he knew that his sins had been washed away by the blood of Jesus, he now saw that he could still be very self-assertive, proud, or vindictive in trying circumstances. The blood had dealt with the sin, and now the cross was beginning to deal with the man.

Freed From the Slavery of Sin

Jesus said, "Truly, I say to you, every one who commits sin is a slave to sin. The slave does not continue in the house for ever; the son continues for ever. So if the Son makes you free, you will be free indeed" (John 8:34-36). This freedom came at a great price, but it was a price that Jesus paid for us. Through baptism into his death, we are freed from the slavery of sin. Through the power of the cross—exercised in faith every day—we can know, in an ever-growing way, the dignity and joy of being beloved sons and daughters of God.

The Name of Authority

Living the Christian life consists of more than experiencing the power of Jesus' blood to wash us clean of sin. It involves more than experiencing the power of his cross to put to death sin patterns in our lives. It also includes the assurance that Christ is with us to overcome the obstacles we face in knowing God's peace and love. In the name of Jesus, we can take authority over the forces in our lives that seek to rob us of our freedom and dignity as Christians. Just as it was true of the blood and the cross, so too with the name; it is God's work, not ours. Jesus told his disciples: "All authority in heaven and on earth has been given to me" (Matthew 28:18). It is by *his* authority that we can know victory.

We might be tempted to think that seeking power in the blood of Jesus, in his cross, and in his name are all doctrinal points of teaching that depend primarily upon our intellectual exercise. There is a danger of this happening if we start to think that it is up to us to figure God out. It is important for us to understand that these sources of power are revelations given to us by God in his mercy—revelations found in scripture and in the Christian tradition. It is also important for us to examine our own lives to see how these sources of power can work in us to bring about our growth and maturity in the Lord.

What's in a Name?

To the ancients, a name was not merely an identifying label, but a revelation of a person's character and his or her role in society. It was the name that both defined and revealed the inner workings of the individual. When a person's name was invoked, that person's character and authority were considered to be present as well. In this sense, it was like an attorney acting in the name of his client, or an ambassador acting in the name of his country's leader.

In Hebrew, the name "Jesus" (*Yeshua*) means "Yahweh saves." When the angel revealed to Joseph the nature of Mary's pregnancy, he told him, "You shall call his name Jesus, for he will save his people from their sins" (Matthew 1:21). It was a revelation of the saving mission of our Lord—a guarantee from God that the long-promised salvation was soon to occur. God was about to save his people from their sin.

In his letter to the Philippian church, St. Paul quoted an early Christian hymn extolling the power of Jesus' name. The hymn speaks of Jesus'

humility and love, which moved him to empty himself and become "obedient unto death, even death on a cross" (Philippians 2:8). The words go on to show how, because Jesus gave up his life to fulfill God's plan of salvation, the Father exalted him, and "bestowed on him the name which is above every name, that at the name of Jesus every knee should bow, in heaven and on earth and under the earth, and every tongue confess that Jesus Christ is Lord, to the glory of God the Father" (2:9-11). Jesus' name has power and authority because Jesus himself has been given all power and authority.

When we call on Jesus' name in faith, we unite ourselves with him and we acknowledge his authority over all things. We place ourselves under his authority and protection, asking him to be present to us and to save us. Scripture promises that "every one who calls upon the name of the Lord will be saved" (Romans 10:13; Joel 2:32). Because Jesus has defeated sin and death for us, we now have the right to call upon him and to experience his authority over strongholds of anger, fear, isolation, and confusion. In the name of Jesus, we share in the victory of his cross.

Rejoicing in the Name

At the last supper, Jesus told his disciples, "Whatever you ask in my name, I will do it, that the Father may be glorified in the Son" (John 14:13). He promised them further that they would know joy as a result of their calling on his name: "If you ask anything of the Father, he will give it to you in my name. [Until now] you have asked nothing in my name; ask, and you will receive, that your joy may be full" (16:23-24).

The first Christians experienced the authority and power of Jesus' name in a very real sense and, just as Jesus had told them, they knew a greater joy than they had known before. In Jesus' name, people were healed (Acts 3:6-8; James 5:14-15);

demonic power was broken (Luke 10:17; Acts 16:16-18); and the believers were united in the name of Jesus (1 Corinthians 1:10).

Like the early church, as we call upon Jesus' name, presenting all our needs and concerns to him, and placing ourselves under his loving care, we too will know joy and freedom. In the end, our joy will be complete only when we are in God's presence for all eternity—worshipping him face to face and delighting in his love. But here on earth, he has given us his name—his presence and his inheritance—as a foretaste of everything that awaits those who trust in the power of his name to protect and deliver them.

Victory through the Name

Mike and Nancy (the couple whose witness we have been sharing) learned to experience the power of Jesus' name more fully as they sought God's wisdom on how to deal with Mike's cancer.

Their experience of the power of Jesus' blood and cross led them to a sense of gratitude that could only be expressed in deeper worship. With their growing realization of the power of the name of Jesus came an increased understanding that worship involves not only what someone does at a specific time and in a specific place, but who someone is as well. Prayer became for them a relationship, not a work; a joyful, loving act, not a difficult labor. It meant coming into God's presence, experiencing his love, and receiving what the Father, Son and Spirit want to give.

But this lesson was not easily learned. There were times when their trust in the Lord was stretched almost to the breaking point. Any sign of further decline in health could set off a chain reaction of thoughts and fears in Mike's mind. The specter of a prolonged, painful death would loom large, casting a shadow over his heart and darkening his thoughts. Dwelling on the rift that had opened between his brother and himself could cause pain and anguish that were sometimes beyond his control. Furthermore, Mike found himself in a new position in which he had to allow Nancy to care for him in a deeper way than ever before. This threatened his pride and sense of self-sufficiency. For her part, Nancy often felt as if she were carrying both of their burdens all by herself, and it weighed heavily on her.

Taking Authority in Jesus' Name

In these situations, they had to learn to take authority in Jesus' name over the fear or anger that confronted them. They would call on the name of the Lord—even say Jesus' name out loud—and place their faith in Jesus' promise that he was always with them to comfort and strengthen them, to give them guidance. Over time, they began to see changes.

For years, Mike had a tendency to wake up at night in a state of anxiety, worried about some impending problem, something left undone, or even with some foreboding of catastrophe. As he continued to call on Jesus' name, however, Mike found himself instead waking up with a song of worship in his heart. He also found himself whistling or humming or even singing hymns of worship during the day, songs that elevated his thoughts to God and filled his heart with joy.

Nancy saw her own life change as well. Knowing God's compassion for her has made her more compassionate toward others, even people whom she used to find hard to accept. She has found a greater ability to help Mike on his more difficult days, and feels that they have grown closer than ever before in their 38 years of marriage. Both Mike and Nancy acknowledge that it was only by relying on the power of Jesus' name that any of this could have come about. And, like the disciples, they are beginning to experience a joy that no one and no circumstance can take from them (John 16:22).

Is God's Power Limited?

What Mike and Nancy have experienced is very precious to them. It is a deep work of healing and renewal which they can only attribute to God's love and mercy. Knowing the cleansing power of Jesus' blood to free them from guilt gave them confidence that they could know his love more deeply. Through the power of the cross, long-standing patterns of sin fell away; the truth of Christ living in them took firmer hold. Through Jesus' name, they found themselves able to face with confidence challenges and difficulties that would have overwhelmed them earlier.

God's power is not limited, his arm is not too short to save. As St. Paul asked: "He who did not spare his own Son but gave him up for us all, will he not also give us all things with him?" (Romans 8:32). In the blood, the cross, and the name of Jesus, God has indeed given us "all things." Our redemption from sin, the gift of the Holy Spirit, the church and her sacraments, and the promise of life everlasting in God's presence, all flow from these truths. Clearly, God has not abandoned his people; he only waits for us to come to him and to receive all the gifts and graces he wants to shower down upon us. In faith and hope, let us approach him and humbly receive from him our inheritance as his chosen and dearly loved sons and daughters.

Christ Lives in Me

Just as with the blood of Christ, the power of Jesus' cross is something available to us through faith. Calling on the power of the cross is not like reciting an incantation which magically dispels our problems. Rather, it is a movement of the heart and mind to affirm our faith in the truth that in baptism we were made partakers of Jesus' death and resurrection. When a situation arises in which we find ourselves tempted by angry or fearful or anxious thoughts, we can say with St. Paul: "I have been crucified with Christ; it is no longer I who live, but Christ who lives in me" (Galatians 2:20). This precious truth speaks not only of our freedom from sin, but also of Christ's loving presence within us. It can give us the strength to withstand any temptation and ultimately know the victory of Jesus' resurrection. We may not feel particularly free the moment we call on the cross, but by faith we can have confidence that God will always hear the prayers of his people and bring them freedom according to his perfect plan (Luke 18:7-8).

Calling on the Cross of Christ

Listed below are various titles given to the cross in the traditional Litany of the Holy Cross. Take some of these titles to your prayer and ask the Lord to open the eyes of your heart more fully to the treasures and promises given us through this wonderful sign of our salvation.

Holy Cross, hope of Christians, save us.

Holy Cross, pledge of the resurrection of the dead, save us.

Holy Cross, way of those who have gone astray, save us.

Holy Cross, consolation of the poor, save us.

Holy Cross, restraint of the powerful, save us.

Holy Cross, refuge of sinners, save us.

Holy Cross, trophy of victory over Hell, save us.

Holy Cross, rest of the afflicted, save us.

Holy Cross, heralded by prophets, save us.

Holy Cross, preached by apostles, save us.

Calling on the Blood of Christ

Much has been said about the power of Jesus' blood to free us from guilt, bring us into the presence of God, and comfort us in times of difficulty. Saints and theologians since the dawn of the church have contemplated this great truth and sung its praises. The following invocations are taken from the Litany of the Precious Blood, a prayer that reflects the riches of the church's dwelling on this wondrous gift of God.

Blood of Christ, price of our salvation, save us.
Blood of Christ, without which there is no forgiveness, save us.
Blood of Christ, Eucharistic drink and refreshment of souls, save us.
Blood of Christ, river of mercy, save us.
Blood of Christ, victor over demons, save us.
Blood of Christ, help of those in peril, save us.
Blood of Christ, relief of the burdened, save us.
Blood of Christ, solace in sorrow, save us.
Blood of Christ, pledge of eternal life, save us.
Blood of Christ, most worthy of all glory and honor, save us.

The Word of Redemption

The following list—which is far from exhaustive—contains some of the more central passages from scripture and the Catechism of the Catholic Church which speak of the power of the blood, the cross, and the name of Jesus.

BLOOD

Scripture

Since we have confidence to enter the sanctuary by the blood of Jesus, by the new and living way which he opened for us through the curtain, that is, through his flesh, and since we have a great priest over the house of God, let us draw near with a true heart in full assurance of faith, with our hearts sprinkled clean from an evil conscience and our bodies washed with pure water. (Hebrews 10:19-22)

Catechism

Jesus is at the same time the suffering Servant who silently allows himself to be led to the slaughter and who bears the sin of the multitudes, and also the Paschal Lamb, the symbol of Israel's redemption at the first Passover. Christ's whole life expresses his mission: "to serve and to give his life as a ransom for many." (CCC, 608)

CROSS

Scripture

We know that our old self was crucified with him so that the sinful body might be destroyed, and we might no longer be enslaved to sin. (Romans 6:6)

For Christ also died for sins once for all, the right-eous for the unrighteous, that he might bring us to God, being put to death in the flesh but made alive in the spirit. (1 Peter 3:18)

Catechism

The cross is the unique sacrifice of Christ, the "one mediator between God and men." But because in his incarnate divine person he has in some way united himself to every man, "the possibility of being made partners, in a way known, to God, in the paschal mystery" is offered to all men. (CCC, 618)

NAME

Scripture

God has highly exalted him and bestowed on him
the name which is above every name, that at the
name of Jesus every knee should bow, in heaven and
on earth and under the earth, and every tongue confess that Jesus Christ is Lord, to the glory of God
the Father. (Philippians 2:9-11)

Catechism

Jesus' Resurrection glorifies the name of the Savior
God, for from that time on it is the name of Jesus
that fully manifests the supreme power of the "name
which is above every name." The evil spirits fear his
name; in his name his disciples perform miracles,
for the Father grants all they ask in this name.
(CCC, 434)